Be The Change

BE
CALM

BE THE CHANGE: BE CALM

An Hachette UK Company
www.hachette.co.uk

Vie Books, an imprint of Summersdale Publishers Ltd
Part of Octopus Publishing Group Limited
Carmelite House
50 Victoria Embankment
LONDON
EC4Y 0DZ
UK

www.summersdale.com

Printed and bound in China

ISBN: 978-1-80007-412-5

Substantial discounts on bulk quantities of Summersdale books are available to corporations, professional associations and other organizations. For details contact general enquiries: telephone: +44 (0) 1243 771107 or email: enquiries@summersdale.com.

Permission has been sought for the Stanley Rosenberg breathing exercises on pages 113 and 119.

Be The Change

BE CALM

Rise Up and Don't Let Anxiety Hold You Back

MARCUS SEDGWICK

illustrated by THOMAS TAYLOR

CONTENTS

Introduction

You weren't born worrying.

You weren't born worried.

*And you definitely aren't
"the type who worries".*

How can I say that? You may well have picked this book up precisely because you feel you are "a worrier". It might seem such a basic part of you that you think you must have been born like that. But you weren't. *No one is born worrying.* There is no "type who worries"; because while it's entirely normal to worry sometimes, the more permanent state we call anxiety is simply something we learn to do, like riding a bicycle. And just like riding a bicycle you can get so good at it, you can do it without even thinking about it. That's part of the problem.

Worrying is a habit. Like any habit, you can do it without even being aware of it. But I have good news! The first piece of good news is that you are already on the way to breaking

this habit, and I can say that with certainty because you have *noticed* that you are worrying and have decided to do something about it. The simple fact that you've picked this book up shows that you have become aware of the problem, and I'm guessing are determined to stop worrying. And I have more good news! Like any habit you acquire in life, the habit of worrying can be changed. And that's what this book is going to help you to do.

Who am I? I'm someone who used to worry a lot. I did it for much, much longer than you, so you might think the habit would have been too hard to break after all those decades of "practice" at it. But I did, and to do it, I used a lot of the ideas in this book.

You can do it too because anyone can Be the Change.

You can BE CALM

How to use this book

This book is designed to be read from the beginning to the end, rather than just dipping in and out. You'll get the most out of it if you read it from cover to cover at least once. Don't worry if it takes you a little while; we don't all read at the same speed, and it's not a race. Once you have read it through, you can go back and reread parts that you've forgotten or want to go over again.

That being said, this is a book about not worrying so much! So don't stress about it – just use it how you want to use it – do what's right for you.

Chapter 1

What is anxiety?

If you're reading this book, the chances are you are already all too familiar with anxiety – that terrible feeling of worry and dread that seems to never end. You sense that something bad is going to happen, and you can't seem to stop yourself from thinking about it...

Anxiety is a word with a long history, because anxiety has been around for as long as human beings have. The word "anxious" itself comes from a Latin word *anxius*, which in turn comes from an even older word *angere* which means to choke, to tightly squeeze or to press hard.

Possibly even just reading that description of the hidden meaning of the word ANXIETY has made your body react in some way. Maybe you recognize feeling as if you can't breathe properly or of your stomach seeming to rise up into your throat. If you do, that's a good thing.

What? Wait!
How can that *be good?*

Well, it's because one of the most important tools to use in beating anxiety is this: your body and how it's feeling. While it's not good if your body is reacting in this way – with a beating heart or clammy hands – it really *is* good news if you're already learning to spot these clear signs of worry, because with them, we're going to help you reduce your anxiety and live your life more happily. We're going to help you be calm.

Anxiety vs worry

We all know what worries are but what's the actual difference between worry and anxiety? Is the second one just a fancy word for the first one?

No! There are many specific differences. Here are just a few of them:

* **Worries tend to be short term; anxiety lasts for longer.**

* **Worries tend to be over specific things, anxiety is more general, often without focus.**

* **Worries tend to be over realistic concerns; anxiety tends to get out of control.**

* **Worries are felt more in our thoughts; we feel anxiety throughout our bodies (more on this later!).**

These are technical distinctions; in this book we will use the terms more loosely and interchangeably.

All in the mind?

When we think about anxiety, we mostly think about the mind. We focus on the negative thoughts we're having, the fears and worries that are circling around and around in our head, which we just can't seem to put a stop to. While a lot of this book is going to talk about what happens in the **mind**, we're also going to talk about the **body**.

That's because to beat anxiety, we need to learn to listen to not just what our minds are telling us in the form of thoughts but what our bodies are telling us too, in the form of symptoms.

So, we're going to jump right into our bodies now, and learn...

Chapter 2

Signs of anxiety

How to spot anxiety

Before we can learn how to Be Calm, we need to learn about anxiety, and not just in a general sense but how it presents itself in your body. This is important because we can't do anything about something we are unaware of. But as we saw at the start of this book; you are already on the way to breaking your habit of worrying, because you're reading this book. You are aware! And once you can spot anxiety in yourself you can do something about it.

Remember that old word – *angere*? It's the source of many related words, such as anger, angst, anguish... none of them nice! Forms of this word can be found in many languages meaning things such as choking, strangling, pressing, squeezing, as well as the idea of something being narrow, or tight. Sounds horrible, right?

As I said before, you might already be aware of how your body reacts when you get anxious but you might not. You might just be so busy worrying about... well, everything it is you're worrying about, that you haven't even noticed the way your body is reacting!

Can you tune into your body? Right now?

Let's take a look...

How in tune with your feelings are you?

First, write down some of the worries that are making you anxious. You could just write one thing, or lots of things. It's up to you.

For example, you might write:

I'm worried about school tomorrow because we have French and I hate speaking aloud when the teacher picks on me. What if I get it wrong and everyone laughs at me?

Or,

I'm scared that my friend is talking about me behind my back. I don't think they like me any more.

You try it now; write some of your worries here:

Now, think about your body. How does it **feel**?

We're not talking about the fears and thoughts in your head, that was for the section on the previous page. This time, we want to know how those uncomfortable things are making you feel *physically*.

So, for example, you might write:

My chest feels tight.

Or,

My shoulders are hunched and tense.

You try it here; write down anything you noticed about your body.

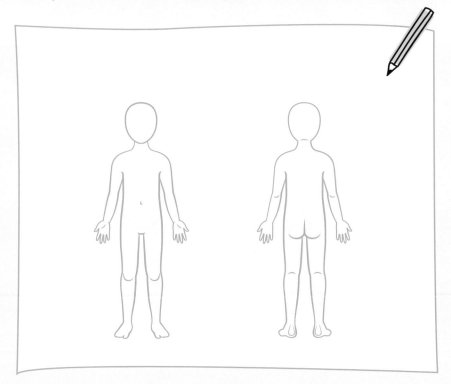

Did you manage to write down how your body is feeling? If you did, congratulations! If not, don't worry; many people are not really that in touch with how their body is reacting to things. That's normal, because our bodies are the place we live, and it's a bit like the idea about the goldfish who has no clue there's a world outside the tank they're living in – it's hard to "step outside" of yourself and see what's going on.

If you did struggle with that exercise, don't worry! We're now going to take a look at an easy way to find the many ways that anxiety can appear in your body.

An important lesson!

Listen up! This technique is the first step in finding ways to help you get on top of your anxiety. It's a basic tool that we'll be using again and again in this book, so it would be really good if you can try it and learn it. The first time you do it, it might take ten minutes or so to complete but the more you do it, the more familiar you'll be with it and soon you'll find you can do it really quickly.

It's called...

The body scan!

There is a lot of information in books and on websites that can teach you one form of body scan or another, but they are all more or less the same idea – like a detective, you're going to explore how your body is feeling in close detail and see what signs and symptoms you can find. These symptoms aren't just random – they are your body trying to talk to you!

So it's time to listen ☺.

Let's start

First, find a quiet, calm and private space. Your bedroom would be ideal, where you can lie on the bed or sit in a comfy chair. If you're not at home, you could just try to find a quiet place somewhere where you can sit and not be disturbed for a little while.

Take one very deep breath. In through your nose and out through your mouth. Just let it go.

Now close your eyes, and take a few more slow, deep breaths, in and out through your nose.

Next, starting at your head, slowly work your way through your body, and see how it feels.

So, using your head as a starting point.

Are your eyes scrunched tight? Or are you frowning? (This is such a common one you might have a hard time even realizing you are doing it!) Or are there some other signs of unease there? Just take a few moments to tune into your body and notice what's there.

Don't worry about whatever you find...

Remember, right now all you're doing is learning a tool that's going to help you with your anxiety. When you reduce your anxiety, your symptoms will naturally also reduce. So for now, just notice what's there. Maybe, for example, your jaw is clenched tight. Okay, but don't judge it. Don't say; "that's bad!" or "that's scary!" or "oh no!". *Just allow these things to be there, and see how they feel.*

When you've finished with your head, move on to your neck. What's there? Is your neck stiff? Are your shoulders tense?

Steadily, at your own pace, move on through your body;

Arms and hands.

Chest and then abdomen.

Groin, legs and feet.

Remember, don't judge anything, just notice, that's all. It's very simple but with time this process becomes a very powerful tool.

The first time you do this body scan, it might take a longish time but you'll get faster the more you do it. The point of the scan is to become more in tune with your body, to notice when you're anxious and how the anxiety is affecting you.

Now, write down everything you found in your body:

For example:

*My chest is tight, and I feel like
I have a lump in my throat.*

What did you find? Did you find a lot of things? Or a few? Either way, don't worry about what you found – if you are worrying a little now, try to turn this around. These things were there and you didn't know it! Now you do. That means you can actually do something about it. Which is what this book is all about, and we're going to help you reduce these worries, over time.

How anxiety feels

You might have a short list of things from the previous exercise, you might have a long one. Anxiety can express itself in the body in many ways; here's a list of some of them, but you might have experienced more things from doing your body scan that aren't listed here. If so, add them to the facing page:

★ **A rapidly beating heart**

★ **Shortness of breath, or "shallow" breathing**

★ **Chest feeling tight**

★ **Neck feeling stiff**

★ **Shoulders raised or feeling tense**

★ **A feeling of something in your throat, as if it's hard to swallow**

★ **Sweaty palms**

★ **An upset stomach or stomach ache**

Phew! You might
be feeling a little
tense right now, so
let's take a look at
a really powerful
exercise, before we
go any further.

Breathing exercise 1 – Cardiac Coherence

This breathing exercise (sometimes also called 365 breathing) has a fancy name but it's really easy to do. All you're going to do is breathe in and breathe out. (And the name isn't as fancy as all that – cardiac just means it's something about the heart, and coherence here means something is regular and consistent.)

What's the point of that? you might wonder. *I'm breathing all the time!*

True, but Cardiac Coherence breathing is special – it's been tested in lots of scientifically controlled experiments and has been proven to:

* **Reduce stress and calm your mind.**

* **Improve your ability to make decisions.**

* **Reduce "racing" thought patterns.**

* **Increase your ability to focus and listen.**

* **Increase your general intellectual capacity.**

And that's just some of the list and only what this breathing technique does for your *mind*!

For your *body*, it:

* **Calms the heartbeat.**

* **Increases energy.**

* **Reduces the levels of cortisol (the "stress" hormone).**

* **Improves sleep.**

* **Strengthens the immune system.**

* **Reduces blood sugar levels.**

* **Reduces fat in the body.**

* **Reduces pain.**

And this list could go on too. That's not bad for something that takes seconds to learn and only a few minutes to do each day!

The idea is that you breathe in and breathe out for the same amount of time.

Try it:

* **Sit or lie somewhere comfortable.**

* **Close your eyes.**

* **Take a moment to "just be" with yourself.**

Now, here we go:

* **Breathe in for five seconds,* and then...**

* **Breathe out for five seconds.**

And...

* **If you can, do this for five minutes.**

Many people suggest that you try to do this five-minute routine three times a day: when you wake up, at lunchtime and before you go to bed.

That's it! So simple.

*If five seconds seems like a long time, just try it for a short period until you get used to it, and work up to five seconds, which is the proven beneficial time for Cardiac Coherence breathing.

Why not try it now, if you can? I'm going to do it too...

Wow, I feel calmer already.
And while some of the benefits
of this breathing exercise occur
immediately, you get the most benefit
by doing it regularly. Every day,
for three five-minute sessions.

If you really want to perfect it; here's a bit more to know: try to breathe "into" your belly – so that your belly expands when you breathe in and contracts when you breathe out. If you're lying down, you can see if you're doing this right by resting one hand on your belly, just above your navel– make your hand rise up when you breathe in, feel it sink down again when you breathe out. (This "belly breathing" is a neat trick to learn. We'll see why later.)

Cardiac Coherence is AMAZING. It's also sometimes called **365** breathing, because:

3 times a day, you practise breathing deeply for

6 times a minute (the cycle of breathing in for five seconds and out for five seconds), and you do this for

5 minutes in total.

And you do it all **365** days of the year*! Trust me, this exercise alone can *change your life*.

(*You can have a day off every four years, if you like, on February the 29th!)

One scientific study showed that Cardiac Coherence has the *physical* effect of increasing a substance in your body called gamma-aminobutyric acid (GABA), which is great news, because GABA has anti-anxiety effects in your *mind*. We'll look more at how *the body and mind work together later.*

"BREATHE IN
DEEPLY TO BRING
YOUR MIND HOME
TO YOUR BODY."

Thích Nhất Hạnh

Chapter 3

Where does anxiety come from?

This is a huge question but, to put it as simply as possible, life can be stressful at times. For everyone. Ugh. In the long term, our response to stress is anxiety. But why do we have this response?

There is a growing amount of work by psychologists – people who study the way the mind works – that tries to understand our emotions in terms of human evolution. The argument goes that in the millions of years in which human beings were evolving, nothing evolved by chance – that all emotions, *even negative ones*, have a purpose. Even if that purpose seems hidden to us today.

It might feel weird to think that even negative emotions have a point to them. How does it help to be angry, for example? Why on earth did we evolve to worry? But there are reasons – the *evolutionary purpose* of anger is to make people go away from you, to leave you alone. It's designed to protect you, in effect.

Why are we all so anxious?

Think about fear – why do we get scared? Fear is the body's reaction in the face of *actual* danger. Worry, meanwhile, is there to warn us of *potential* danger. Worry is your mind's way of thinking through possible problems in order to avoid getting into dangerous situations in the first place.

Explanations of this kind often use the example of a primitive human going about their daily life – here he or she is pootling about, looking in the forest for berries to eat, and very occasionally being confronted by a hungry sabre-toothed tiger! Now that confrontation is going to cause a reaction of fear – the point of which is to make you run away, with a surge of adrenalin in the body to help you run even faster.

Now consider two types of early humans; one type carries certain genetic information that makes them think about possible dangers that might be *in their future* (such as tigers in the bushes), and the other group doesn't.

The way evolution works is that the people who think through the danger of tigers will on the whole take steps to avoid being eaten, while the bunch who noisily skip through the forest without a care in the world will on the whole get eaten more often. So the first group survive more in general and so pass on this same genetic information to their descendants, who, after a very long time, are us.

It's in this way that worry came about. It was there to help us.

The trouble with worry is that, in the modern world, it has got really out of control. It has become anxiety.

Evolution works over almost unimaginably long periods of time – the mechanisms described above were probably really vital for the not-getting-eaten-by-a-tiger stage of human existence but are less helpful today. The modern world has arrived almost overnight, in evolutionary terms, and the human species hasn't had the time to evolve, to change, to adapt to this new world.

"ANXIETY'S LIKE A ROCKING CHAIR.

IT GIVES YOU SOMETHING TO DO,

BUT IT DOESN'T GET YOU VERY FAR."

Jodi Picoult

External stressors

Every day we are bombarded by information, news and comments and we have responsibilities and obligations the like of which were unimaginable to primitive humans. People who study the history of human beings think we probably evolved to live in small communities, such as 50–150 people; that was our entire world and it was manageable. Compare that with the world we now live in – you go to a school where there are already hundreds, even thousands more people to encounter than that small group our ancestors knew. Plus, we have access not just to the news of our small community but the entire world. And there's no escaping it.

We are overloaded by media of all kinds; scientists are only just beginning to understand the effect the internet is having on us. All in all, life is very busy and while lots of it is fun, some of the things we encounter are stressful. While we can cope with a certain amount of stress, and a small amount of stress can even be fun (for example, watching your favourite football team, going on a roller coaster), too much stress can lead to us being permanently anxious.

So, what can we
do about it? Can we
do something about it?
The good news is yes, we
can, and that's what the rest
of this book is here to do...
We're going to start
in the mind.

Chapter 4

The mind is a funny place

And when I say "funny", I mean strange...
You experience the world through your senses
– all the information your eyes and ears
receive; things you smell, taste and touch
– all these things are taken in by your brain
and then, in some mysterious way scientists
still don't understand, you *think about them.*

Human beings are conscious of their existence; we think about stuff, we form opinions, we believe things. However, the mind is not a totally reliable machine. And while sometimes your thoughts might be accurate, sometimes they may not be.

When we think about worries, it's really important to be able to distinguish FACTS from FEELINGS, because although it's easy to believe that what you are thinking is absolutely true, it's possible you might be getting things a little (or even a lot!) wrong.

So, let's take a look at this.

Fact or feeling?

On page 16, we wrote down some worries. Let's take a deeper look at the way we worry about things. To do that, write down some more of your worries here; anything you are feeling anxious about (it's often very helpful merely to say your problems out loud or write them down, something you might already know if you keep a diary!):

For example, you might say:

There's a maths test on Monday and I'm going to fail it.

Or,

So-and-so is bullying me all the time, and there's nothing I can do about it.

What's bothering you right now? Write some things here:

Let's look really hard at what you have written. How much of what you have written is A FACT? And how much is A FEELING?

FACTS are things like this:

Squares have four sides.

The world is round.

Five times three is 15.

London is the capital city of the United Kingdom.

There's a maths test on Monday.

FEELINGS, on the other hand, are things like this:

I never get any good luck happening to me.

I'm going to fail that maths test.

There's nothing I can do about so-and-so bullying me.

It's very important, when dealing with anxiety, to be able to tell whether something in your head is absolutely true, or whether, just maybe, your worry is running away with itself.

Of course, your feelings will have an element of truth to them. You are probably unlikely to worry that giant killer octopuses are going to come marching down your road blasting everyone with ray-guns (if you are, trust me, we're safe on this one). No, the dangerously powerful thing about anxieties is that they are usually *based in truth*, and on *possible outcomes*.

So, if we look again at some of the worries above:

"There's a maths test on Monday" is a FACT (unless the killer octopuses zap your maths teacher over the weekend, or disintegrate your school), Whereas, "I'm going to fail that maths test on Monday" is not a fact. It's an opinion, it's a FEELING. You don't know *for sure* that you'll fail it. (You might feel very sure that you're going to, but you can't be sure. Maybe it will be easier than you're expecting – this actually happened to me with my A-Level Maths exam!).

Starting to be able to tell the difference between the two is very helpful when we're dealing with anxieties.

Your feelings are valid!

Now, just because we're saying that your feelings, your worries, aren't necessarily the TRUTH, it doesn't mean that we're ignoring them. Neither does it mean you don't have good reason to feel the way you are feeling. If you are being bullied at school, then *of course* this is going to make you fearful and worried a lot of the time. Although it's not fun, you have a right to feel the way you do and, as we saw earlier, what's more, these feelings are your body's way of saying, "Hey, dude! Something's wrong! Let's do something about it!"

This book is designed to help you with your worries, and there's no time like the present, so here are a couple of ways you can try to let your feelings go:

First, as we noted above, simply telling someone what you are worried about can help, as can writing things down, such as in a diary, if you don't feel able to talk to someone just yet. When you talk to people, or write things down, it makes you reflect about the issue that's bothering you. Sometimes you realize as you're speaking or writing that you don't actually think things are the way you've been feeling. Just maybe you have been making things worse than they actually are (more on this in a moment!).

Or, here's a really simple mindfulness practice. One of the first things to note is that you have a right to worry! You're not being silly if you have anxious feelings – they are your mind and body trying to talk to you. So don't be hard on yourself – the first thing to do is recognize and accept your fears for what they are. Buddhist mindfulness techniques can help here.

Take a comfortable, upright sitting posture.

Close your eyes.

Adopt a gentle rhythm of breathing in and out for the same amount of time, maybe a count of four or five.

Then, as you breathe in, name your fear: say in your mind, "I see that I am anxious," or "I recognize that I'm worried." Say whatever works for you. Whatever feels like it strikes a chord.

Then, as you breathe out, say,

"I let this anxiety go,"

or

"I set this feeling free."

That's all! It's really, really simple.

Practise doing this for a few minutes a day, or whenever you need it. The more you practise, the more powerful this tool will become. More on mindfulness and breathing to come!

The reason it's important to be able to tell apart facts from feelings is this; very often, the thing you're worrying about, the thing that you've been worrying about for days, weeks, months even... just doesn't happen.

If you're anxious, it's very possible that you will often think of the worst possible thing that could happen – and this tendency has a fancy name.

It's called...

Catastrophe. What a word! A word that describes total disaster, the very worst possible thing that can happen. Recently, the word has been turned into this verb – catastrophizing – to describe the thing we do when we assume that the worst that can POSSIBLY happen is the thing that WILL DEFINITELY happen.

But how likely is it? How often do earthquakes strike, or airplanes crash? Yes, these things do happen but they are really very, very, *very* rare events in life.

It might help you, if you keep thinking the worst is going to happen, to look at a graph. Imagine we plotted a graph of "what happens when I leave the house". Along the X-axis, we have a scale from "0" meaning "the worst possible thing happened" e.g. a piano fell on me and squashed me flat. The chart goes up to "100" meaning, "the best possible thing happened" e.g. my favourite footballer was waiting to give me a cheque for a million dollars and also told me I'd won the Nobel Peace Prize and had just been voted "World's Best Human Being". Again. Shucks.

Up the Y axis, we have the *total number of times* an event of that type has occurred.

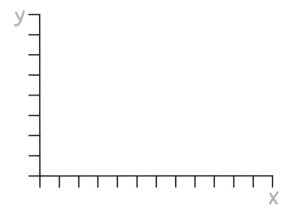

Now, we start going through all the times you have walked out of your front door, and we give each event a number from 0–100 for how bad to how good whatever happened was. Then we add up all the times we gave a score of 0, and a score of 1, and a score of 2, etc. all the way up to 100.

Then we can plot the results on our graph. The chances are it would look something like this:

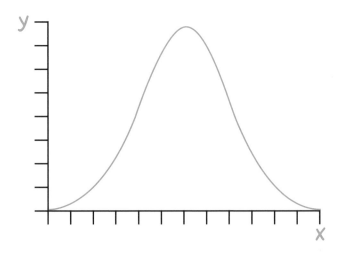

This is a shape called a bell curve (it doesn't look that much like a bell but that's why it's called that, mathematicians, eh?). It appears *all the time* in statistics. It's a really useful shape to bear in mind when you're worrying. That's because what it says is this: most of the time, the thing you're worrying about – in this case, leaving your house because something bad might happen – doesn't happen. Or isn't *that* bad.

Look at the graph. At the left of the x-axis, we have *zero* times that something totally awful happened (i.e., that piano hurtling towards you from a great height), and looking at the right of the x-axis, we also have *zero* times that your favourite football player gave you an award for being a brilliant human being.

In the middle though is a big hump – it's the total of all the times that totally AVERAGE things happened when you left the house; things you maybe gave a score of 40 to (it rained but not much, you missed your bus and so on) or maybe that you gave a score of 60 to (you got a seat on your bus, it was sunny and so on...).

The big bell in the middle is telling you one thing – life is mostly quite boring! Very bad things do happen, but not very often at all. And sadly, really amazing things don't happen that often either. Of course, the shape on the left-hand page is just one example; your bell curve might look more like one of these curves:

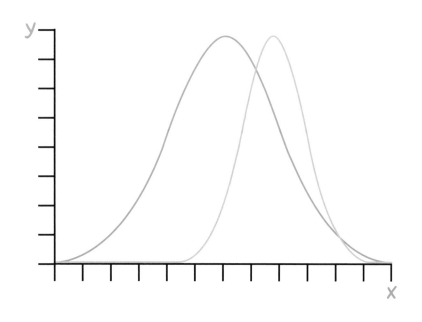

Or other variations, but the thing to remember is the very tiny ends to the graph – extreme events are just that, extremely rare.

To prove this idea to yourself a little more; let's do another writing exercise.

Think back to the past. Let's write down a couple of times that you were worried about something. Try to remember things that you were *really* worried about. You might have trouble thinking of some, or you might find this easy. Write them here:

Now, of these things that you *thought might happen*, which of them *actually* did? It could be that all of them did, or at least a few of them, and so you're now thinking, "There, I told you my life is rubbish!"

If that's the case, there may be a very simple explanation for this – you are *much* more likely to remember the times when bad things actually did happen than the times when you thought something bad was going to happen, and then, in the event, the result was totally okay.

This fact, that we tend to focus on bad things more than good things, is well known to psychologists. The explanation seems to be that it's another way we have evolved – and which protects us – by noticing and remembering bad things more than good ones, because the bad ones might be dangerous, and naturally we've evolved to avoid dangerous things. That's almost the most basic point about evolution; remember, characteristics that get us eaten by tigers will not get "chosen" in the process of natural selection and will not get passed on to our offspring!

You might like to try to prove this to yourself here, by writing down the times in the last couple of weeks you thought something bad was going to happen but it didn't:

You might find this hard. If you do, it only goes to prove the point that evolution has trained us to focus on bad things, so we try to avoid them in the future. We try not to waste the memory space in our minds by remembering all the times that *absolutely nothing interesting* happened, either good or bad. However, it's a good idea to keep working on showing yourself the times when things actually went okay, even though you thought you were completely doomed!

The truth of the matter is this: we are not fortune tellers. (Well, most of us aren't.)

We often think about the future; it's another ability human beings have, to predict and to plan. While sometimes we can be fairly sure of how things will go, life is *unpredictable*. This unpredictable nature of life can in itself make some people feel anxious, and if you're one of those people, remember the bell curve! Mostly, life is just sort of okay, and that's fine.

As we are not fortune tellers, we do tend to think quite a bit about how things will go, and very simply, the way people see the future divides us into these types: OPTIMISTS and PESSIMISTS.

Optimists are people who tell themselves that things will be good, that things will generally work out well.

Pessimists are people who tell themselves that things are probably going to be bad, that life is generally mean and unfair.

The optimists tend to say things such as "look on the bright side" and "every cloud has a silver lining". They say that, even though bad things do happen, it's better not to spend time worrying by assuming that they will. It's better to go through life with a cheery, positive outlook.

Meanwhile, the pessimists think that optimists are foolish types and that it's better to be prepared for the bad stuff that is inevitably going to come. They might say that if you go through life as a pessimist, you're not disappointed when things don't work out as you wanted.

SO, WHICH IS THE BETTER WAY TO BE?

Well, this is complicated, because some studies have shown that optimists live longer, healthier lives, while other studies have found the opposite! Some things do seem to be fairly clear; studies have shown links between pessimism and depression, for example. Equally, other studies have shown that being overly optimistic leads to reduced mental well-being and a greater risk of death at an earlier age!

So, what's going on?

The issue is complicated by a third personality trait – being a REALIST.

Realists are people who (at least as far as is possible) see things as they truly are, not as fantasies of good or bad.

There's an old saying that goes like this:

A pessimist sees a dark, dangerous tunnel ahead.
An optimist sees the light at the end of the tunnel.
But a realist sees a high-speed train.

Meanwhile, a train driver sees three idiots standing on the train tracks.

72

It seems that in us humans, we are not just simply one of these three things: realist, optimist or pessimist. The traits can combine with each other. So, for example, realism can combine with either pessimism or optimism.

So, you can be a realistic optimist or an unrealistic optimist.

You can also be a realistic pessimist or an unrealistic pessimist.

As a quick bonus exercise, can you think of friends or family members who say things like this? Maybe you don't want to write these down where anyone can see, but it can be interesting to think about people who you know and work out which type of person they are. Can you work out which type you are, generally?

So, here's the thing, of these four possible types above, which one generally has the easiest, happiest and also healthiest outcomes in life? Can you guess? Why do you make that guess?

Want to know the answer? Turn the page...

WELL, IT'S THE REALISTIC OPTIMISTS.

Various studies have shown that optimism, balanced with a dose of realism, is the best combination: you go through life generally feeling less anxious but are aware that bad things might happen. When they do, realistic optimists tend to also be more resilient – which means they can accept the bad thing that has happened, and get on with life anyway.

Positive affirmations

Just as we can talk ourselves out of believing in ourselves, we can talk ourselves into believing in ourselves too! This is where affirmations can work wonders. These are useful sayings to repeat to yourself, throughout the day, such as:

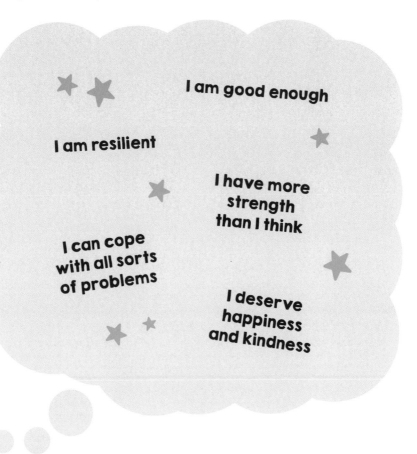

I am good enough

I am resilient

I have more strength than I think

I can cope with all sorts of problems

I deserve happiness and kindness

Write a few of your own here and repeat them whenever you need to give yourself a boost.

"If you are
depressed, you are
living in the past.

If you are
anxious, you are
living in the future.

If you are at peace,
you are living in
the present."

Lao Tzu

Hey, it's been ages since we thought about taking a deep breath, so let's learn another exercise:

Breathing exercise 2 – Square breathing

Square breathing is another incredibly simple technique to calm you down. As with 365 breathing (page 34), it has proven health benefits. Just before we do it, however, it's a great idea to do a very quick body scan, as we learned to do earlier (page 20).

This is for two reasons – first, the point of the body scan is to make you more in tune with your feelings, both physical *and* emotional, and to see that these two things are connected. Second, if you do the body scan before and after each breathing exercise, just a quick check in, you will start to see how even five minutes of breathing can have a powerful effect on you.

So do a quick scan...

... and then let's learn square breathing.

It's really simple; all you do is this:

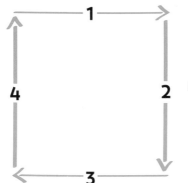

Breathe into your belly for a comfortable slow count, say to 4, 5 or 6.

1

4 Repeat this for a few minutes, as long as you want, or as long as you have time for.

2 Hold for the same amount of time.

3 Breathe out for the same amount of time, and, yep, you guessed it, hold for the same time.

It's called square breathing because it has four equal "sides", and you can visualize yourself breathing your way "around" a square, if you like. To practice, you can even trace your finger around the sides of this square, until you get the hang of it.

Play with the length of time you use. Find a period of time that's right for you, nice and comfortable.

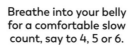

TIP!

You can find free apps for smartphones and tablets that guide you with visuals, sound or even just vibrations through these kinds of breathing exercises. They can make it even simpler to follow and help you to stick to a routine, which is great, because you get much more out of these exercises if you do them regularly, and not just when you're in a moment of crisis, though they can be very helpful then too.

Chapter 5
Storytelling

A quick word about storytelling

I'm a writer. I tell stories for a living. If I do it well, I get paid for it, which is great (and if I don't do it well, I don't eat, which isn't fabulous). But writers aren't the only type of people who tell stories. In fact, we all do it. We all tell stories, whether we think we do, or not. And although this might surprise you, stories can be dangerous!

Have you ever caught yourself telling stories? If you have, you will already know what I'm talking about. If not, it's a good idea to start to recognize when you're storytelling, and since we're looking at anxiety in this book, the stories I'm talking about are the ones you tell about yourself. About who you are and what you're like and what you're good at. And about what's going to happen to you.

These stories are not the facts about you. It's not things like where you were born and what colour your eyes are. We want to consider the things that form the story of our lives.

Let's try an exercise...

Storytelling exercise

We're going to try to write down some stories you tell about yourself.

Think about yourself – what things do you often say about yourself, either out loud or in your head? Have you ever stopped to think about this before? If you haven't, you might find this hard. If you're having trouble, try this: imagine stepping outside of yourself and looking at yourself. You have a superpower – you can see and know *every* thought in this person's head! Be kind, but be honest; what does this person in front of you now always say about themselves?

For example, you might write:

I like spending time with my friends.

Or you might put down:

I'm no good at drawing.

Or:

I'm not strong enough to cope with this stuff!

Have a look at what you've written. Look for two things – how many of the stories you tell about yourself are good, and how many are bad?

Secondly, how many are actually *true*?

For example, are you really bad at drawing? Most people say they are, and when you ask them, they usually tell some story about how someone was mean about something they'd drawn when they were seven or eight. Then they stopped drawing. But were their drawings at that age *really* any worse than anyone else's? Probably not. Drawing is hard, and the people who are good at it as grown-ups are the ones who kept on trying.

However, a story like that, "I'm not good at art", is one you can keep on telling yourself throughout your whole life if you're not careful. Trust me, the world of grown-ups is full of people who told themselves a story like that when they were small, and it just kind of stuck. Which is a shame, because a different story, such as – "I'm finding art hard but so is everyone else. I enjoy it so I'm going to keep on trying" – might have seen them have a different life where they have a hobby, or even a profession, that they really enjoy.

Be careful what you think!

Make sure you catch yourself when you're telling stories about yourself and, just as we saw with facts and feelings earlier, learn to distinguish what kind of story you are telling.

Try to limit the negative stories you tell about yourself; try to replace them with different or better ones. Stories can be dangerous but they can also be very empowering. The latest work in the field of neuroscience (the study of the brain and how it works) shows us that the brain changes. Not just that – it changes *all the time*. This is a relatively new concept called *neuroplasticity*, and what that means is that the brain is physically making new connections between neurons (the cells that make up the brain) all the time. It's how you learn a new skill – no one is born knowing how to play the piano but anyone can to some extent with enough effort.

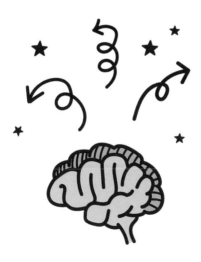

Scientists who study the brain have shown that *even your thoughts themselves* can create new connections in the brain. Experiment after experiment has proved that *merely thinking about something* is almost as powerful as actually doing that thing. This is why athletes use visualization techniques of themselves clearing all their hurdles, or taking the ski run perfectly, or whatever it might be. If pianists just *think* about playing the piece they're going to perform, they actually get better at it, as if they had done the practice for real.

It's amazing stuff, now all verified by science but it can be either good or bad. For example, if you repeatedly think negative things in your head, you will actually *reinforce* those pathways in the brain. Think of it like a cart going down a muddy track; with every trip, the ruts in the track get deeper. This means it gets harder to drive down the track in any other way. So the more you think depressing thoughts, the harder it will be to stop. As I said right at the start of this book, anxiety is a habit.

The good news is that this process applies to good thoughts as well as to bad ones. What's more, as you start telling yourself good stories in place of bad ones, the connections in the brain that you made with the bad ones will weaken, while the good ones will get stronger and stronger. The effects of all this are only just being discovered but it's really exciting and positive news. It means you can literally use your thoughts to "rewire" your brain, making your mind a happier and more positive place to live. You can change your habits. Anyone who tells you that people can't change is wrong. You can; you just have to believe you can.

You are what your thoughts make you.

You are your thoughts. (So be careful what you think!)

86

Self-compassion break!

Compassion is the art of being kind to people – of caring for them and listening to them. Of being their friend. But you can practice self-compassion too!

Try this activity. For just three minutes every day, close your eyes and repeat some of the following things to yourself, happily and calmly. Really try to mean them; reach out to yourself as if you were reaching out to a friend in need of support.

How often do you say such things to yourself? Do you ever do it? It's very likely you don't. It's equally likely you tell yourself bad things about yourself. So give yourself a break and for just three short minutes every day, tell yourself some good stories about who you are!

I am kind

I am strong enough

I am a good person

I am calm

I can cope with whatever comes my way

I am human – anyone can make mistakes

On the next page, complete this list with whatever you feel is good and right. Be nice to yourself! Be understanding!

Magical thinking

Magical thinking is a special type of storytelling. In order to cope with worries that you have, you might have started to tell yourself little stories like this:

If I see three red cars on the way home, everything will be okay.

Or:

If I reach that lamp post before that bus does, the bad thing I'm worrying about won't happen. But if I don't reach it, it will.

Once again, it's worth spotting if you are doing this sort of thing. These magical thoughts are *not* facts, and you shouldn't start to treat them as if they are.

It can be harmless if you don't take this stuff too seriously, but it's easy to give these thoughts more weight and meaning and then it can start to rule your life. The counting thing (e.g. "if I see three red cars...") is very common, especially among teenagers – it's the sort of thing we don't admit doing, but which many of us are doing or have done at some point in our lives. That's why, although lots of books and websites on anxiety will include tips using counting to distract you from your worries, I suggest you do these kinds of activities with care.

For example, some people suggest that if you're really worrying about something you can calm yourself using distraction, by counting all the blue things you can see, or counting backward from a hundred. Or simply counting sheep to help you sleep. The trouble is that while these techniques can work in the short term, they can encourage obsessive counting behaviours in us too. And you're already anxious enough!

So instead of counting, why not try this mindfulness technique? You can do it whenever you need to and wherever you are.

Simply take a deep breath in through your nose, and then let it out through your mouth, nice and relaxed.

Now, start to notice all the sounds you can hear. Don't count them, just say: there's a bus going by, there are birds singing, there's the buzz of the fridge, whatever it might be, depending on where you are. Keep going until you have done all the things you can hear.

Next, what can you smell? Can you smell anything? Notice any smells – and then name them!

Now, what can you feel physically? Do you feel cold? Warm? Hot? Are you touching anything? What does it feel like? Can you feel any of your clothes against your skin? And if you do, how do they feel? Are you sitting on anything? What does that feel like? How is your body in general?

You don't need to judge anything at all – this exercise is simply about noticing things, and naming them. As you do this, you still your mind. By the time you have spent five minutes doing this exercise, you should feel calmer, having stopped your mind whirring around and around, thinking about all the stuff that's been troubling you. Instead, you come into the present moment and into your body and you see what is real.

Right, time for another breathing technique! As before, ideally do a really quick body scan before you start and another when you're finished.

Breathing exercise 3 - 4-7-8

This one is a little more complicated, but just like the other techniques we've learned a growing number of studies are proving that such breathing techniques are effective against anxiety. Not only that, they are safe and easy to use. They also don't just help the mind, they also have proven benefits for the body (which is where we'll be going right after this exercise).

Breathe in through your nose for a steady count of four.

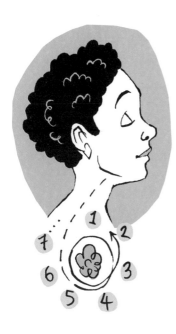

Hold your breath for a count of seven.

Breathe out for a count of eight, but *through your mouth*.

As before, keep this cycle going for three or four minutes, or whatever you can manage right now.

That's it!

4-7-8 breathing is based on breathing techniques from the ancient Eastern practice of yoga, and has proven effective against anxiety, in particular, helping to calm a racing heart. This seems to be triggered by the breath-holding part. Many people find it especially helpful when they are having trouble getting to sleep.

z z Z Sleep on it

Sleep is another really important thing to tackle when you're anxious. The chances are that if you are worrying about something all the time, you are having problems with sleep, which is another great reason to do these breathing exercises regularly and right when you get into bed is the perfect time. With more sleep you will be better able to cope with whatever is happening in your life; with too little sleep, problems can seem bigger, and it can be harder to deal with them.

If you really can't get stuff out of your mind before going to sleep, try writing things down. The end of the day is a great time to keep a diary, and it doesn't have to mean you write pages and pages every night. A single line is great sometimes. Just write down what's worrying you and tell yourself that by writing these things down, you give yourself permission to stop thinking about them. You give yourself permission to have a good night's sleep. That alone can do you wonders – my mother told me lots of things when I was young, but the single truest one of them was this: *don't judge things when you're tired.*

When you're tired, everything seems worse. Molehills become mountains; glitches become catastrophes. So when you're having a really bad moment, it's always a good idea to ask yourself if you're tired. Is it late? Have you had an exhausting day? Well *of course* everything seems worse, so get some rest. I'm not asking you to pretend your problem isn't happening. I'm not telling you it isn't real. I'm just saying, when you're tired, it will automatically seem worse; so try this deal with yourself: don't judge how bad the problem is now. "Sleep on it", get some rest, look at it again in the morning. Then at least you will have a truer image of what is going on.

As we saw before, it can be hard to be sure that our feelings and the facts agree with each other. Here are two important things to realize:

First, your mind affects your body. If you worry, your body will show it; the beating heart, the sweaty palms and so on.*

And secondly, the body affects the mind.

> ***This is how lie detector machines work – they measure the changes in the body as a result of stress – in this case, the stress of (potentially) being caught lying.**

That's what the rest of this book is about, because when it comes to anxiety, thinking about what goes on in the mind (as important as it is) can only get us so far.

We need to think about what happens in the body too.

To do that, let's start by thinking about animals!

Chapter 6

What animals can teach us about anxiety

It might seem strange to think about animals in connection to worrying, but there's a lot we can learn by observing animals, by thinking about what they do, and especially about what they *don't* do. In this chapter we're going to let animals help us to reduce our anxiety.

Animals are wise. They don't necessarily know they are. But they are.

Think about a wild animal, maybe even watch one on a nature programme on TV – it could be a gorilla sitting preening with its mate, it could be a wolf running, on its own or with a pack. It might be a deer grazing on a hillside.

Watch it a few times (in your head if you're imagining this); watch it closely.

Look at this lion here:

Write down some things you notice about the animal; whole sentences, just adjectives if you like, whatever you think of:

★ **The lion [for example] is very strong.**

★ **It's fast.**

★ **Beautiful.**

Have a look at what you have written. I would be very, very, very surprised if you have written "anxious". Maybe if you thought about a tiny mouse, it might be acting nervously, looking this way and that, to see if a bigger animal is about to catch it. But anxiety is a long-term thing and here's the big difference between us and animals – animals do not get anxious. (The only time they do is in cases of captivity, when they're in small cages in zoos, for example, and start to display symptoms of anxiety, or mental distress.)

A wise man once said to me: look at a lion, think about a gazelle – do they worry? Do they obsess about what is coming tomorrow?

Do they ask themselves if they have a right to exist?

Do they feel guilt?

Or shame?

It's worth thinking about.

Now, we are not animals. We've seen how anxiety is a response to the stress of modern life, because of our super-aware human brains trying to figure everything out all the time, trying to *control* everything all the time. But it can help to look at your dog or cat and try to live with a bit more of the freedom – mental freedom – that they do. Watch them lying on their bed, just breathing. Living in the present moment, not worrying about the future, not obsessing about the past. Sit with them for a while. Slow down. Be more like an animal... It's good for you!

> **Being around animals is calming, it's good for you. Research has shown that single people who live with a dog are happier and healthier than single people who live totally alone. Now there is an explanation to why – when mammals hang out together, their nervous systems "co-regulate". What this means in practice is that they help to calm each other down. Make each other feel safe. This works because their nervous systems "talk" to each other, sending all sorts of signals through tiny facial expressions, body language, and so on. The incredible thing is that this happens *between species* – so just being with your dog is good for you. You probably already knew that ☺.**

Yawn! Have you ever noticed that sometimes, when one person in a group starts yawning, people around them do too? This isn't necessarily because they have all suddenly decided they are bored or tired. This so-called "contagious yawning" can be a sign that the nervous systems of you and the people around you are *co-regulating*. Scientists don't yet agree on what this means exactly, but chimpanzees do it too, and there is some evidence it indicates closeness, and empathy, between individuals in a group.

Silly activity!

Why don't you see if, without telling anyone, you can get your family or friends to start yawning around you? Fake a yawn (you'll probably find you don't have to fake it after the first couple!) then wait and see what happens. If you succeed, it's proof that your nervous systems are talking to each other, directly. Cool!

Animals in the wild do not display anxiety, and that's despite the fact that many of them live in stressful situations. While the lion may be top of the food chain on the African savannah, the gazelle it preys upon isn't as lucky. So why isn't the gazelle *anxious* with all this danger around?

Look at this gazelle being caught by a lion. After a long, hard chase, the gazelle is finally caught and the lion pounces on it. In a final desperate measure, the gazelle employs a trick that some animals use in such situations: it plays dead, it stops fighting and just lies there. Perhaps much of the time, this trick doesn't work and the animal gets eaten anyway. From time to time though, it seems to confuse the lion, who doesn't attack it and kill it but instead seems to get bored. After a short while, it wanders off. Crazy. But that's not the point of the story.

The point of this story is what the gazelle does next; it stands up, groggily, and then it starts to tremble all over, shaking violently for maybe 30 seconds. Then it suddenly recovers, and runs off, as good as new.

Shake it off!

Biologists are not sure about what this is all about, but one idea is that the gazelle is releasing the trauma of the attack. Once it trembles, it's gone. It literally gets the trauma out of its system. We humans, on the other hand, are all too good at holding on to the bad things that happen to us. We can let them start to guide our thoughts and behaviours for the future.

So maybe we can learn a little something from animals. (There is even a therapy called TRE, or Tension and Trauma Release Exercises, that is based on this observation.) But we can also learn from our own bodies too, which is why learning and repeating the body scan is so helpful.

Are you lucky enough to go horse riding? Horses are amazing! Their hearts are huge, and beat slower than ours do. One thing that has been discovered is that when you spend time with a horse, your heart rate slows down to try to match the horse's, and the effect of that is that it calms you down. How does this work? Well, mammals' hearts have electromagnetic fields around them, and the heart of a horse has an electromagnetic field that is a huge five metres in diameter! It's a powerful thing to be in the influence of. And very good for you.

The limits of thought

So, why is there a limit to the work we can do to calm our body with our mind alone? It's very simple – the body "thinks" things faster than the mind does.

What do I mean by this?

To understand, the first thing we need to do is think about the human body. You've probably picked up at school, or somewhere else, that human beings work like this: the brain is some kind of computer, doing all the thinking and organizing, and the body is a machine, that follows the brain's computer-like instructions.

This model has been around for about four hundred years, since the days of a French thinker called René Descartes. He was a smart man, but unfortunately, this picture is wrong. This is an area of science in which old ideas are now being challenged, and new ones fought over, but there are some exciting discoveries being made.

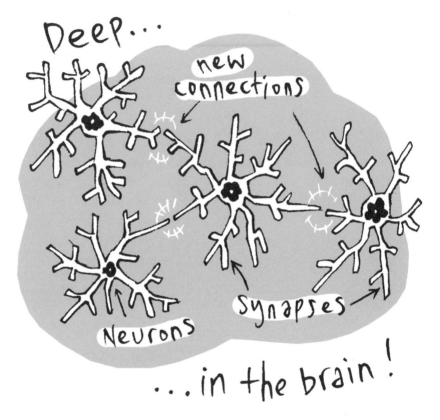

For one thing, the brain is not like a computer. It's probably wrong to compare the brain to anything else at all – because it is very special. It's now known that the brain is not a fixed piece of hardware like a computer, it changes and grows all the time; in fact, as we saw earlier, every single thought you have is making or reinforcing neural connections.

For a second thing, there is an idea that human brains are composed of three different areas.

Our most primitive mechanisms are things generally out of our conscious control, like our heart rate. Also, we don't have to think to breathe, we just do it. While you can control these two things to an extent, your body is continually controlling dozens of similar mechanisms in your body, such as adjusting the release of various hormones, over which you have neither knowledge nor control.

These functions are controlled by what's called the "reptilian brain" because the structures found here were once thought to dominate the brains of reptiles and fish.

Next, there is the "limbic brain", which appeared in mammals, a later form of life than reptiles. It's from this mammalian brain that basic things such as nurturing, rearing, caring, bonding and emotions come.

Finally, there are the parts of the brain – the latest addition to what's inside the skull – unique to humans and perhaps some apes – in which we have self-aware, abstract thought. We are conscious. This part of the brain is called the "neo-cortex".

(This "triune brain" idea, that the human brain is composed of three parts, was introduced by Paul D MacLean in the 1960s. In fact, it is a simplification; while the reality is vastly more complicated, this basic breakdown does help us think about certain aspects of human beings.)

What does this have to do with anxiety? Well, that "unconscious" reptilian brain is thinking and acting, reacting to things such as danger and stress milliseconds before your conscious human brain has even got out of bed. Milliseconds might not sound like much, but it's enough to have you run with fear, or lash out in anger, or wet yourself with fright before you even know what's happening.

"I just didn't think!"

... you might say later, after some sudden action.

No, your conscious mind didn't but that really primitive part of your brain did – before "you" knew what was happening, it acted to *protect* you (yes, even in wetting yourself, an evolutionary trick to make your body as light as possible before running away from that rampaging tiger!). Your body is always working to protect you. It's always trying to talk to you – to send you messages – even with anxiety. It's a good idea to listen!

And that's not the end of the story about brains...

Chapter 7

You have two brains!

The second brain

Here's something that might surprise you – you have two brains! See, you always knew you were smart, right? The second one is smaller than the one you already know about, and it's somewhere that might surprise you – it's in your belly! There's even a third one, which is even smaller, and that's on your heart.

Scientists are just beginning to discover that the gut has millions of neurons – the same cells that we used to think were unique to the brain and which we do our "thinking" with. In fact, the heart only has around 40,000 neurons, but the gut has around *500 million*, so many that some people are starting to refer to it as a "second brain". Suddenly it makes sense why our language has always been full of sayings like "a gut feeling" or "my heart told me" and so on. There is a very strong argument to say we don't really know where the mind ends and the body starts, or vice versa.

For all these reasons, we need to check in with our bodies and, as much as it's good to work on anxiety using our minds, it's vital to work on our body's relationship to anxiety too.

The Basic Exercise

I think it's time for another exercise. A very simple one, in fact. It was invented by a man called Stanley Rosenberg, who over the last 40 years or so has been a pioneer in various amazing body therapies. This exercise is so simple you might doubt what it's doing, and to really see it working, you need to have become reasonably good at checking in with your body using the body scan (page 20).

Body exercise 1 – the Basic Exercise

Follow along with the illustrations and instructions. It's worth going through the directions a couple of times or watching more than one video because although this exercise is very simple, there are a couple of small but important things to get right.

Body Scan ...then... look straight up!

Now...

look over one way...

First, do a quick body scan. What is your body feeling? What is it saying? Do you have tension in your neck? Do you just feel anxious, maybe as if you're fizzing, wound up? Don't try to fix anything, or worry about it. Just notice.

then the other...

Body Scan again.

Eyes only!

Look out for...

a sign.

Here's the Basic Exercise in detail:

Now, lie on your back and rest your
head on your interlinked hands.

Look straight up.

Now, very gently, and without turning your head
(this is harder than it sounds!), move just your eyes
to look to one side, right or left, you choose.

Move them as far as is comfortable,
no further, this shouldn't hurt.

Maybe find a spot on the ceiling in the
right place and look at it. Now...

Wait...

Wait some more.

You can slowly count if you want to but
all you need to do is wait.

Eventually, after maybe 30 seconds, or a minute, your body will give a small sign that something has shifted (see below for what that thing is). This sign might be that you swallow. It might be that you yawn. You might feel a shift in some other way and, if you've really been out of touch with your body, it might be hard to spot at first.

When you feel the yawn or swallow or whatever it is, shift your eyes back to the centre, and then move them to the other side and do the same thing... wait...

When you get the "release" on the other side too, you're done.

That is, apart from the body scan, because the final thing is to check in with your body again and see if anything has changed. When I do this exercise, I notice very clearly that I feel "lighter". My brain feels less "chewy"; I feel, in one word, calmer. But see how you feel.

The Basic Exercise is very subtle. So subtle in fact, that you might not think it can possibly be doing anything. We have been brainwashed in the modern world that for drastic changes to happen, you have to take drastic action. "No pain, no gain" and all that. However, when it comes to the body and anxiety, sometimes very gentle things can have a very profound effect. So, when you first do the Basic Exercise, as with the breathing exercises, you might not think that anything very powerful is happening. But give them time and they can change your world.

So how does the Basic Exercise work?

A few cutting-edge researchers have been studying one very special nerve in the human body. It has a very boring name, the 10th cranial nerve, and a *slightly* more interesting one, the vagus nerve. The name "vagus" comes from the Latin meaning "to wander" and that's because this nerve goes a long way through the body, from the brain all the way down the gut, in fact.

These researchers are starting to make some amazing discoveries about the vagus nerve. For one thing, we now know that not only does the vagus nerve take messages from the brain to the gut, it also takes messages from the gut to the brain. It also carries messages from the chest and lungs.

This is why, when you do belly breathing, you calm your mind, because it sends signals via the vagus nerve to your brain, to tell you everything is okay.

Let's state that again, because it's worth it:

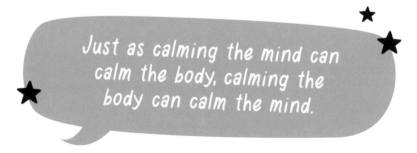

Just as calming the mind can calm the body, calming the body can calm the mind.

The mind and body are inseparable. We can't even say which is which, really. A mind cannot exist outside of a body and a body without a mind is, well... probably dead.

Let's have another exercise by Stanley Rosenberg.

Body exercise 2 - Half Salamander

This exercise works on the vagus nerve again.

Find somewhere you won't be disturbed and sit upright.

As before, check in with your body with a body scan and see how you are feeling.

Are you anxious? Fizzy? You could even give it a score – a number out of ten, to compare with after you have done the exercise.

Now, gently tilt your head to whichever side takes your fancy, as if lowering your ear to your shoulder.

Don't twist your head or point your face towards your shoulder, simply lower your head sideways.

Do not lift your shoulder to your ear; leave your shoulders down, and just imagine you are trying to get your ear as close to your shoulder as is comfortable. Don't strain! Don't push any further than is nice to do.

Now, move your eyes up and to the side, to the corner away from where you are moving your head.

Wait!

Maybe hold it there for 30 seconds or so.

When you're ready, slowly come back to the starting position, looking straight ahead.

And then...

Repeat the whole thing on the other side.

Hold...

And release when you're ready.

That's it!

How do you feel now?

Check in with that feeling – check your score again. When I do this, I usually find the "fizzy" feeling in my body has sunk from a 6 or 7 to a 3 or 4. Not bad for a minute's work.

There are various versions of this exercise. I really like the Half Salamander ☺. Every time I do that I feel as if someone has "cleaned" my brain a little. And in a way they have – it has helped to reset my nervous system, and the "someone" who did it, was me, which is a great feeling in itself! But this is just one more method and there are countless techniques that you can use that work with your body to really get to the heart of your anxiety.

Chapter 8

A bag of calming tricks

We've already made a start in learning how to cope with anxiety in the earlier chapters with exercises such as the Half Salamander and breathing techniques. This chapter will take things even further. Here you'll find a toolbox of techniques you can do to help yourself with anxiety, in simple and practical ways.

Breathing!

Do not underestimate how much regular breathing exercises can do for you. If you can make these things a habit, so that you almost no longer need to think about doing them, they can make a huge difference to your daily life. We've taught you some simple ones here in this book but there are dozens of different breathing exercises out there. To keep things simple, if I were to suggest just one, it would be making cardiac coherence (365 breathing, see page 29) a part of your life – just five minutes, three times a day; that's something easy to fit into your day.

Exercise

Exercise is great, if you can do it. Regular exercise has been shown over and over again to really combat anxiety, depression and more. It causes the body to release natural substances such as endorphins, which make you feel great. Of course, not everyone can exercise, but even if you have a health problem which prevents you from running or swimming, for example, you can try other methods, such as...

Meditation and mindfulness

We touched on mindfulness earlier. It's a huge subject and happily is becoming something that more and more people are aware of. Once these ancient techniques were only known in Asia but now more and more people are making them a part of their daily lives.

Meditation is an extremely powerful tool to combat anxiety if practiced regularly, and anyone can do it. You don't have to become a Zen monk overnight! But, once again, research has now shown the benefits on the mind and the body of regular meditation.

There are loads of great books out there, and you can also find great apps to guide you through them to get you started, or help you stick to a routine. It doesn't have to be boring or hard work!

Yoga and tai chi

These are very gentle exercises, which again originated in Asia, but which are now practiced throughout the world. They combine a bit of meditation with movement, and they are suitable even if you cannot do strenuous sport. Both can really work wonders with consistent practice, helping you to feel centred, grounded and strong. To feel calm.

While using the techniques we've talked about here will go a long way to you leading a calmer, happier life, there are also things you need to do less of as they can trigger feelings of worry and anxiety and simple things you can do more of that will leave you feeling happier and calmer. Here are some of the main ones.

What to do more of

 Smiling, playing and laughing...

Anything that makes you smile or laugh is wonderful. Not just because it feels great in the moment but because it lowers your stress. For example, laughing regularly has been shown to reduce the levels of cortisol in your body – the so-called stress hormone. Also, simply smiling releases endorphins and that reduces stress too – it even works when you don't feel like smiling! Try it. Fake a smile, tip your head back, stick your chest out and make yourself laugh. Even if you feel silly doing it, you'll feel the positive effect it has.

Playing can take your mind off your worries, giving you a break from what's happening elsewhere in your life, and play can take many forms. Just goofing about with friends, for example, can be as joyful as actively playing a game. And playing can take many forms; from sports to board games to role-playing games to all sorts of hobbies. The exact numbers vary, but research has shown that children laugh many, many more times a day than adults do! There are a lot of reasons why this might be, but it's worth remembering that laughter has been shown to be really, really good for you. It has all sorts of immediate beneficial physical effects inside your body. There's even a form of yoga called laughter yoga – which combines the best of both of these wonderful things! So, find more ways to have fun.

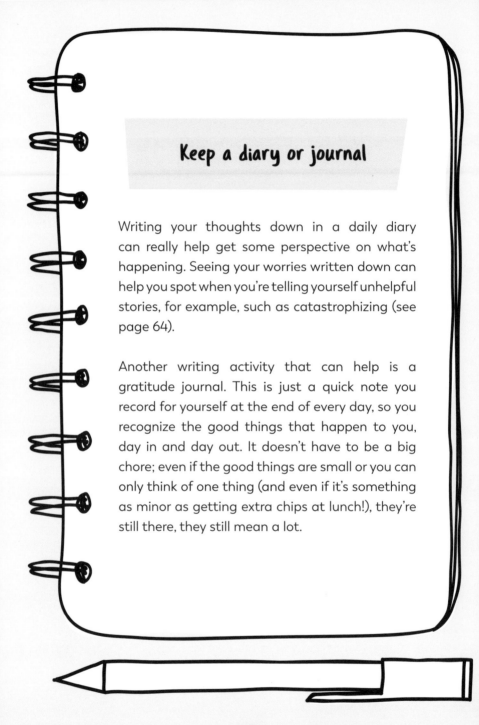

Keep a diary or journal

Writing your thoughts down in a daily diary can really help get some perspective on what's happening. Seeing your worries written down can help you spot when you're telling yourself unhelpful stories, for example, such as catastrophizing (see page 64).

Another writing activity that can help is a gratitude journal. This is just a quick note you record for yourself at the end of every day, so you recognize the good things that happen to you, day in and day out. It doesn't have to be a big chore; even if the good things are small or you can only think of one thing (and even if it's something as minor as getting extra chips at lunch!), they're still there, they still mean a lot.

Self-compassion

This is a big one!

> It's not your fault that you're feeling anxious.

I can't say this enough, and it's worth telling yourself this, over and over again. Your body is simply reacting to stressful times by sending you signals of anxiety. It's a natural process and it's not your fault. You are not weak, or broken, or stupid for worrying. These things are natural. So give yourself a break, don't beat yourself up.

Don't forget the self-compassion exercise we met earlier in the book (page 87) – give yourself a five-minute boost every day. There are also more great exercises on self-compassion to be found online. Giving yourself a boost doesn't mean you have to become a big-head, over-fond of yourself. It just means you know how to be kind to yourself, to treat yourself as you would like other people to treat you.

> Be kind to yourself.

Do good things for other people, especially if they are struggling

This can really shift your focus out of your mind and your problems and back into the world. It gives you perspective, as well as the reward of seeing your friend or family member feeling better.

As a quick activity, you could write a list of the most important people in your life then alongside their names write down something you can do to make their lives easier. It doesn't have to be huge – giving a compliment, making a cup of tea or even a hug can all make a difference! Just something nice that they will appreciate. Even just writing your list will make you feel good; doing it will make you feel even happier.

Enjoy the small things

Life doesn't always have to be about the big moments, the incredible things, like amazing birthday parties or holidays. Lots of life is quite quiet, but you can really enjoy it much more if you take pleasure from even the small things – a joke with a friend, a chat with your mum, a favourite book, a meal that you really like. Try not to rush through your life – stop and enjoy the moment, whenever you can. Being connected to the present moment is grounding – it helps to keep you calm.

 ## Do more creative things

"Flow" is a word that has become trendy over the last few years for when creative people get "in the zone"' – but artists and writers have known for centuries that time seems to work differently when you are really into the piece of art you're making. If you're an artistic type, great! If you're not, don't worry – you can become one. This isn't about how "good" you are at your chosen artistic activity – it's about "losing yourself" in the process. Sketching, painting, knitting, whatever it is, once you really focus on it, your mind will calm down; you'll stop those anxious thoughts that might otherwise have been bothering you.

Start the day on a good note

How you start your day can really set the tone for the rest of the day so consider how you want to kickstart your mornings. Maybe you can add in a little ritual every morning, some breathing or yoga, or some realistic but optimistic thoughts. Maybe you can play a favourite song, one that makes you feel "up"!

Perhaps you can get out into nature, even into your back garden; it can be really calming. Remember that there is a big and beautiful planet out there, aside from the silly things that people sometimes do. The planet is always there, giving you air to breathe, food to eat, water to drink and beauty to look at!

Can you walk your dog? Feed your cat?

Is there a little thing you can do every morning that never fails to make you feel good?

EFT – Emotional Freedom Technique, or "tapping"

Tapping is one of those things you need to try to believe – how can tapping your fingertips around various points on your face help with anything? But it does! Tapping has been around for a few years now, but recently it's been tested in the lab, and it's been shown, for example, to reduce the levels of cortisol (that old pesky stress hormone) in the body by over 40 per cent – this is way above what many therapies have achieved in similar experiments. All you do is tap certain key points on the head and face, while repeating out loud the thing that is bothering you. A minute or two of this and suddenly... you find the thing isn't bothering you nearly as much, or even at all! The points align with acupressure points from Eastern traditions, and there are lots of sites on the net and books to explain what to do. It's free, you can do it yourself, it's fast, and it's REALLY effective.

Stuff to avoid, or cut down on

Outside or hidden stresses

I've tried to show you how the mind responds very strongly, and unconsciously, to what's going on in the body. So, while you might not *think* you are being affected by the scary film you're watching, if we wired you up to a machine to measure signs of stress, your heart rate and so on, we might see a different story. Remember, if you are increasing or creating stress in your body, you are in turn putting stress on your mind, even if you're not aware of it.

That's why, if you're going through an anxious period in your life, you might want to cut down on things like stressful films, games, etc. If you're having fun, that's wonderful! But if they're making you more stressed than happy, then maybe a break would be a good idea.